D1287511

My First Animal Library

Coyotes

by Cari Meister

Bullfrog Books

Ideas for Parents and Teachers

Bullfrog Books let children practice reading informational text at the earliest reading levels. Repetition, familiar words, and photo labels support early readers.

Before Reading

- Discuss the cover photo. What does it tell them?

- Look at the picture glossary together. Read and discuss the words.

Read the Book

- "Walk" through the book and look at the photos. Let the child ask questions. Point out the photo labels.

- Read the book to the child, or have him or her read independently.

After Reading

- Prompt the child to think more. Ask: Coyotes live all over North America. Have you ever seen one? Was it alone or in a pack?

Bullfrog Books are published by Jump!
5357 Penn Avenue South
Minneapolis, MN 55419
www.jumplibrary.com

Library of Congress Cataloging-in-Publication Data

Names: Meister, Cari, author.
Title: Coyotes / by Cari Meister.
Description: Minneapolis, MN : Jump!, Inc., 2018. | Series: My first animal library | Series: Bullfrog books | Includes index. | Audience: Ages 5 to 8. Audience: Grades K to 3.
Identifiers: LCCN 2017040251 (print)
LCCN 2017043178 (ebook)
ISBN 9781624967559 (ebook)
ISBN 9781624967542 (hardcover : alk. paper)
Subjects: LCSH: Coyotes—Juvenile literature.
Classification: LCC QL737.C22 (ebook) | LCC QL737.C22 M442 2018 (print) | DDC 599.77/25—dc23
LC record available at https://lccn.loc.gov/2017040251

Editor: Jenna Trnka
Book Designer: Leah Sanders

Photo Credits: Marc Bruxelle/Shutterstock, cover; Jim Cumming/Shutterstock, 1; KeithSzafranksi/iStock, 3; Marg Woods/Design Pics/Getty, 4; Geoffrey Kuchera/Shutterstock, 5, 23ml; Warren Metcalf/Shutterstock, 6–7, 23mr; Matt Knoth/Shutterstock, 8, 23bl; Bryant Aardema/Shutterstock, 9; Michael Francis Photo/Age Fotostock, 10–11; National Geographic Creative/Alamy, 12–13, 23br; Thomas & Pat Leeson/Science Source, 14–15; Martin Froyda/Shutterstock, 16; Jed Packer/Shutterstock, 17 (foreground); Galyna Andrushko/Shutterstock, 17 (background); mlharing/iStock, 18–19, 23tl; Danita Delimont/Getty, 20–21; jlwhaley/iStock, 22; Ad _ hominem/Shutterstock, 23tr; Jack Nevitt/Shutterstock, 24.

Printed in the United States of America at Corporate Graphics in North Mankato, Minnesota.

Table of Contents

Howl and Hunt

AAOOO!

A coyote howls.

It is dusk.

It is time to hunt.

The pack howls back.
They will hunt together.

A coyote has
a long muzzle.

muzzle

It can smell well.

A coyote has long legs.
It smells a mouse.
It runs very fast.

11

Its teeth are sharp.

It grabs its prey.

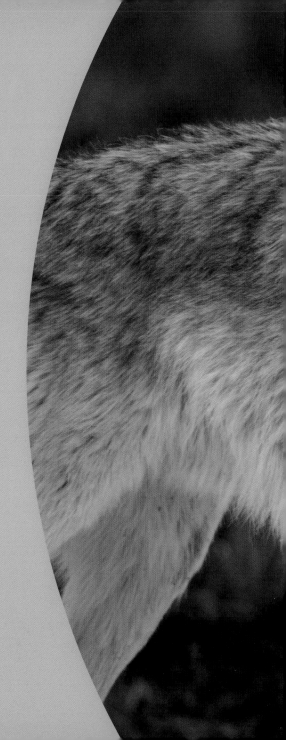

prey

What do coyotes eat?

Almost anything.

Rabbits. Fish.
Berries.

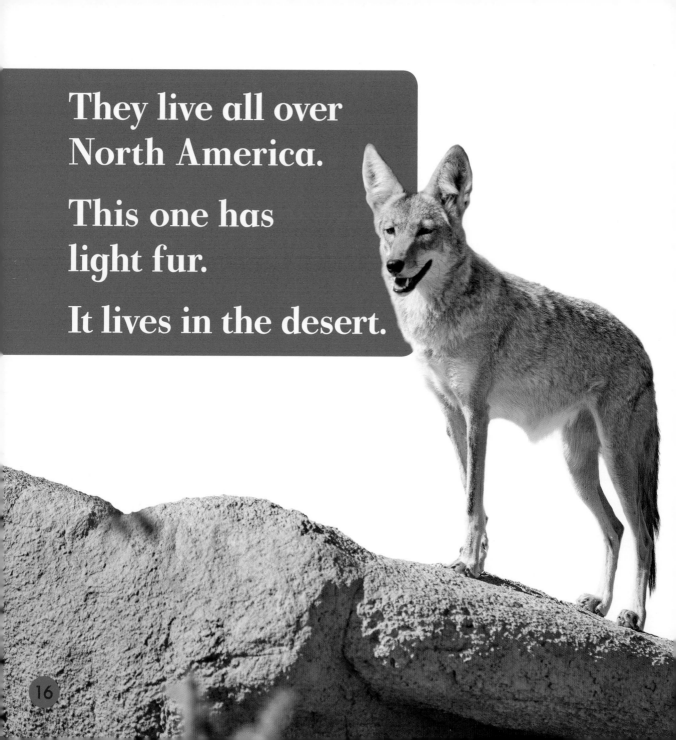

They live all over
North America.

This one has
light fur.

It lives in the desert.

This one has dark fur.

It lives in the mountains.

17

See the pups?

They are new coyotes.

They are safe by the den.

They will learn to hunt.

Parts of a Coyote

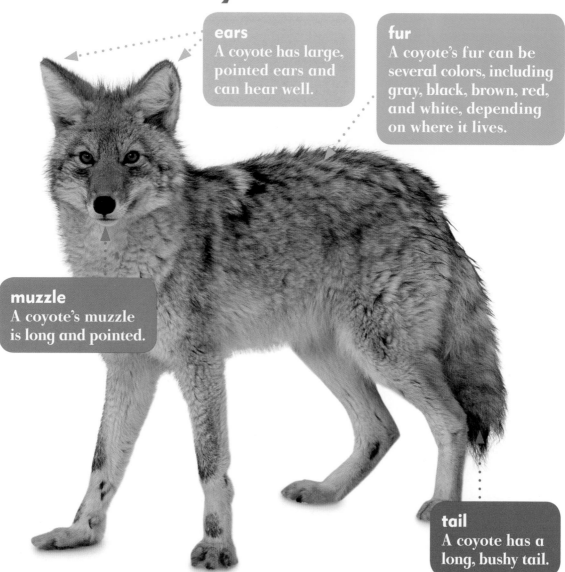

ears
A coyote has large, pointed ears and can hear well.

fur
A coyote's fur can be several colors, including gray, black, brown, red, and white, depending on where it lives.

muzzle
A coyote's muzzle is long and pointed.

tail
A coyote has a long, bushy tail.

Picture Glossary

den
The home of a wild animal.

North America
The continent that includes the United States, Canada, Mexico, and Central America.

dusk
The time of day after sunset when it starts getting dark.

pack
A group of similar animals.

muzzle
An animal's nose and mouth.

prey
An animal that is hunted by another animal for food.

Index

To Learn More

Learning more is as easy as 1, 2, 3.

1) Go to www.factsurfer.com

2) Enter "coyotes" into the search box.

3) Click the "Surf" button to see a list of websites.

With factsurfer.com, finding more information is just a click away.